Stone, Lynn
Predators: Fish.

DATE DUE	BORROWER'S NAME

FISH

PREDATORS

Lynn M. Stone

Rourke Publications, Inc.
Vero Beach, Florida 32964

Edited by Sandra A. Robinson

PHOTO CREDITS

© Chip Matheson: cover, pages 8, 10; © Alex
Kerstitch: pages 7, 15; © Lynn M. Stone: title
page, pages 4, 13, 21; © Tom and Pat Leeson:
pages 12, 18; © Breck P. Kent: page 17

Library of Congress Cataloging-in-Publication Data

Stone, Lynn M.
　　Fish / by Lynn Stone.
　　　　p.　cm. — (Predators)
　　Includes index.
　　Summary: Describes different kinds of predatory fish, where
they live, and how they catch their prey.
　　　ISBN 0-86625-436-6
　　1. Fishes—Juvenile literature. 2. Fishes—North America—
Juvenile literature. 3. Predatory animals—North America—
Juvenile literature. [1. Fishes. 2. Predatory animals.] I. Title.
II. Series: Stone, Lynn M.　Predators.
QL617.2.S73　　1993
597'.053—dc20　　　　　　　　　　92-34489
　　　　　　　　　　　　　　　　　　　　　　CIP
　　　　　　　　　　　　　　　　　　　　　　AC
Printed in the USA

TABLE OF CONTENTS

Fish as Predators   5
Fish Weapons   6
How Fish Hunt   9
Sharks   11
Other Saltwater Fish   14
Freshwater Fish   16
Fish of Fresh and Salt Water   19
Fish and People   20
Saving Fish that Hunt   22
Glossary   23
Index   24

FISH AS PREDATORS

A shark's jaws are well-known for their rows of sharp, white teeth. They are teeth made for grabbing, tearing and killing.

The shark is an expert at killing, and it needs to be. After all, without flesh on which to feed, a shark would starve.

The shark is the best-known of fish **predators**— the fish that must hunt and kill to survive. However, nearly all fish in North American waters, fresh and salt, are also predators. They feed on victims known as their **prey.**

A spectacular leaper, the tarpon is a large predatory fish in the Gulf of Mexico

FISH WEAPONS

Most **predatory** fish kill with their jaws and teeth. Some of the largest, sharpest teeth of North American fish belong to sharks, barracudas and the freshwater muskellunge.

The giant billfish—marlins, sailfish and swordfish—are toothless. They use their spearlike bills to stab other fish before eating them.

The lamprey, which looks like an eel, kills its fish victims slowly. The lamprey attaches its sucking mouth to the side of a fish. Its teeth cut through the scales and flesh. Then the lamprey sucks its victim's blood and fluids through the wound.

The viper moray eel displays savage jaws

HOW FISH HUNT

Sunlight does not go through water very well. A fish probably never sees prey more than 100 feet away. It's dark down there! How does a fish find distant prey?

Fish sense prey—and danger—by feeling sound waves that travel through the water. Sharks also have a great sense of smell. They can smell and swim toward tiny amounts of blood in the sea.

Fish, of course, do use their eyes to find nearby prey. Some fish can leap from the water to grab low-flying insects.

The shark's sense of smell
helps it find injured prey

SHARKS

Sharks of many sizes and kinds, or **species,** live along the Atlantic and Pacific shores of North America. American sharks range in size from less than one foot in length to more than 60 feet.

In North American waters, the famous great white shark can be 20 feet long and weigh 3,000 pounds. It eats fish, seals, birds and sea turtles.

Sharks have large jaws and powerful, slim bodies. A few species of large sharks are dangerous to people.

The blue shark, like the white shark on the cover of this book, is a large and dangerous species

The brightly colored rainbow trout is one of the most popular game fish

*A favorite game fish of the Southeast, the snook likes brackish water—
a mix of fresh and salt waters*

OTHER SALTWATER FISH

The shark is indeed a very good hunter. However, the oceans are the **habitat,** or home, of other predatory fish, too. Snook, tarpon, redfish, sea trout, bluefish, halibut, grouper, barracuda, mackerel and tuna are just a few of the ocean dwellers.

The largest fish usually hunt alone. Many other fish, both hunters and hunted, travel together in groups called **schools.**

Schools of small fish are attacked by big, hungry fish. Sometimes the commotion caused by these attacks brings more trouble for the little fish. When the ocean surface looks like it's boiling with silvery fish, sea birds rush to the feast.

A school of barracudas hunts for ocean prey

FRESHWATER FISH

Ponds, lakes and rivers are the habitats of predatory fish, too. The largemouth bass is one of the most common.

This cousin of the bluegill and **bream** is well-named. Its large mouth helps it satisfy its large appetite for other fish, frogs, insects, salamanders, mice and ducklings.

Less common—but no less predatory—are the long, toothy northern pike and its relative, the muskellunge.

The most beautiful of North America's freshwater predatory fish are trout. The names of three kinds—cutthroat, golden and rainbow—suggest their bright markings.

The largemouth bass has a hefty appetite for fish, frogs and other animals

FISH OF FRESH AND SALT WATER

Several species of predatory fish travel between rivers and the sea. Trout born in rivers along the coasts often travel to the sea. Later they return to fresh water to lay their eggs.

Salmon are close relatives of trout. They also swim from rivers to the sea. As adults at sea, salmon are fierce, sharp-toothed predators.

The largest of the six species of American salmon is the king, or chinook. It often weighs more than 50 pounds. Five species live off the Pacific coast and the sixth type lives off the Atlantic.

The chinook, or king salmon is the largest of five species of salmon on the Pacific coast

FISH AND PEOPLE

People with fishing poles and fishing boats are predators. They make big, predatory fish suddenly become prey. For a sport fisherman, the biggest, hardest fighting fish are the best prey.

Fish that fight well and strike **lures** are called **game,** or sport, fish. Lures imitate a fish's real prey.

Game fish thrill sport fishermen by striking lures in the same savage way they attack live prey. Many fish—rainbow trout, largemouth bass and tarpon among them—make spectacular leaps when hooked on a lure.

The predatory largemouth bass becomes prey for a wiser predator

SAVING FISH THAT HUNT

Commercial fishing is the catching of large numbers of fish to sell. That kind of fishing has reduced many populations of fish.

Polluted water and dams that stop fish migrations along rivers have been harmful to fish, too. Digging with machines in shallow, saltwater bays has destroyed fish nurseries, the places where fish begin to grow up.

Oceans, lakes and rivers look huge. It is easy to believe they will always have plenty of big, slashing fierce fish. Not true. Without more attention to clean water, and building and fishing limits, we will lose some of our prized predatory fish forever.

Glossary

bream (BRIHM) — popular nickname in South for freshwater sunfish

game (GAME) — an animal that is hunted or caught for sport

habitat (HAB uh tat) — the kind of place in which an animal lives, such as a freshwater lake

lures (LOORZ) — objects hooked to the end of a fishing line. Lures imitate the natural motions of prey

predator (PRED a tor) — an animal that kills another animal for food

predatory (PRED a tor ee) — having the habits of a predator

prey (PRAY) — an animal or animals that are hunted for food by another animal

schools (SKOOLZ) — groups of fish, usually of one kind, that travel together

species (SPEE sheez) — within a group of closely related animals, such as trout, one certain kind or type (*rainbow* trout)

INDEX

barracudas   6, 14
bass, largemouth   16, 20
billfish   6
commercial fishing   22
dams   22
eggs   19
fishermen   20
game fish   20
jaws   5, 6, 11
lamprey   6
lures   20
muskellunge   6, 16
nurseries   22
people   11, 20
prey   5, 9, 20

salmon   19
   king   19
schools   14
senses   9
sharks   5, 6, 9, 11, 14
   great white   11
size   11, 19
sound waves   9
tarpon   20
teeth   5, 6
trout   16, 19
   rainbow   16, 20